Raven *and* River

For the Jeffers: Nancy, Denny, Jamie, and Kimmi— great friends in the Great Land! With Love—N.W.C.

Rave on, skoomkum bird!—J.V. Z.

Text Copyright © 1997 by Nancy White Carlstrom
Illustrations Copyright © 1997 by Jon Van Zyle
All rights reserved

Published by University of Alaska Press
P.O. Box 756240
Fairbanks, AK 99775-6240
Originally published by Little, Brown, and Company 1997

Library of Congress Cataloging-in-Publication Data

Carlstrom, Nancy White.
 Raven and river / by Nancy White Carlstrom ; iIllustrated by Jon Van Zyle.
    p. cm.
 Summary: Raven and the other animals try to awaken the frozen river to
the coming Alaskan springtime.
 ISBN 978-1-60223-150-4 (pbk. : alk. paper)
[1. Ravens—Fiction. 2. Rivers—Fiction. 3. Alaska—Fiction. 4.
Spring—Fiction. 5. Animals—Fiction.] I. Van Zyle, Jon, ill. II.
Title.
 PZ7.C21684Rav 2011
 [E]—dc22
                                    2010051460

Cover design by Dixon Jones
Text set by Taya Kitaysky

This publication was printed on acid-free paper that
meets the minimum requirements for ANSI / NISO
Z39.48–1992 (R2002) (Permanence of Paper for
Printed Library Materials).

Production Date: May 1st 2018
Plant/Location: Printed in Guangdong, China
Job/Batch Number: 81814/EPC 714277

The paintings in this book were done in
acrylics on untempered Masonite panels.

SECOND PRINTING

Raven and River

By Nancy White Carlstom

Illustrated by Jon Van Zyle

University of Alaska Press
Fairbanks

Raven
knowing
swoops out of winter into spring,
circling, circling.
He gurgles and burbles,
Like a river flowing.

R-r-rawk, r-r-rawk quiver
Wake the sleeping River.

Red squirrel
listening
skitters up the highest spruce.
She searches this way, that way,
back again.
Bright eyes sparkle,
like a river shining.

Chit-chit shimmer
Wake the sleeping River.

Ruffed grouse
strutting
rearranges feathers.
He beats his wings,
like a river humming.

Thum-thum thither
Wake the sleeping River.

Wolf
rising
climbs out of her own sleep
up the steep cliff.
She raises her head and howls, then takes off,
like a river running.

Yowl-yowl shiver
Wake the sleeping River.

Snowshoe hare
twitching
leaps to the air.
In two-color coat,
she bounds over familiar paths,
like a river dancing.

Run-run hither
Wake the sleeping River.

Bear
yawning
gets up from dreams of fish.
Big-pawed and groggy,
he enters the light,
like a river turning.

Slap-*slap* dither
Wake the sleeping River.

Beaver
waiting
is not surprised.
For in his old winter lodge
he feels the ice begin to shift,
like a river moving.

Crick-crack sliver
The River The River.

Raven circles and circles and circles.

R-r-rawk, r-r-rawk quiver
Chit-chit shimmer
Thum-thum thither
Yowl-yowl shiver
Run-run hither
Slap-slap dither
Crick-crack sliver
Circle for the Giver
The River The River

River squints through eyes of ice.
She stretches and stretches and stretches,
waking up
breaking up.

R-r-rawk, r-r-rawk quiver

Then River
shimmers for red squirrel,
hums with ruffed grouse,
runs after wolf,
and dances with snowshoe hare.

River turns over with fish for bear
and moves in a new home for beaver.

And Raven—
Raven dips and soars
dips and soars
cutting the bright blue cloth of a sky
tumbling
flying
swooping
crying.

Together
Raven and River
gurgle and burble and roll their *r*'s

R-r-rawk, r-r-rawk quiver
Circle for the Giver
Rr-rip-rip Raven Rr-rip-rip River
Rippling rippling rippling

Raven flying
River flowing
Free

Author's Note

Raven and River are part of our daily lives here in Fairbanks, Alaska, where I live. The Raven, so black against the white Alaska landscape in winter, is much more than a scavenger. I have seen him tumble through a blue sky, soar fluidly over the treetops, and land at my feet, cocking his head as if to say, "Of course, I know it is forty below zero. So what?"

Likewise, the River is a strong presence. In the winter, it freezes and becomes a highway to snowmachines, skis, and dogsleds. In one place, called the "ice bridge," even cars and trucks cross over the thick ice.

By the first week of May, one can usually see huge ice chunks crashing dramatically downstream. Spring is one short month of melting snow, oozing mud, and budding leaves.

During this, the time of breakup, it is common to hear the Raven's throaty gurgle, sounding like running water, as it flies over the changing landscape. The Raven's call always reminds me of the waking river.

—N. W. C.